Understanding Neurodiversity

An information handbook for parents / carers, educators & sports coaches

Jenny Cluning

First published by Busybird Publishing 2024

Copyright © 2024 Jenny Cluning

ISBN
Print: 978-0-6454446-1-2

This work is copyright. Apart from any use permitted under the *Copyright Act 1968*, no part of this publication may be reproduced, stored in a retrieval system or transmitted in any form or by any means, electronic, mechanical, photocopying, recording or otherwise, without the prior written permission of Jenny Cluning.

The information in this book is based on the author's experiences and opinions. The author and publisher disclaim responsibility for any adverse consequences, which may result from use of the information contained herein. Permission to use any external content has been sought by the author.
Any breaches will be rectified in further editions of the book.

Cover design: Busybird Publishing

Layout and typesetting: Busybird Publishing

Busybird Publishing
2/118 Para Road
Montmorency, Victoria
Australia 3094
www.busybird.com.au

Foreword

I first met Jenny in 2012 when she called and asked me to present an INPP (Institute for Neuro-physiological Psychology) Teacher Training course. That meeting was the start of a wonderful friendship which still continues to this day.

Whilst getting to know Jenny, I also had the privilege of getting to know her husband and three sons. Her two youngest boys required ongoing learning support, and Jenny left no stone unturned in an effort to help her boys find the best solutions to their difficulties and to help them reach their full potential.

I was a teacher prior to doing a master's degree in special education, and subsequently completed my post-graduate training in Neuro-developmental Immaturity through INPP, Chester, England, and the Johansen Individualised Auditory Stimulation programme training in Denmark with the late Dr Kjeld Johansen.

In my years of working with children, I have met many committed parents who want to help their children – but none so determined as Jenny. Hers is a story of love, devotion, perseverance and patience in accessing every type of medical and educational support for her boys. This can be read in her first book, *Building Bright Futures*.

I have walked part of that journey with Jenny. I trained her in the use of the INPP Method for assessing and treating Neuro-motor Immaturity, as well as training her to become a provider of the Johansen Individualised Auditory Stimulation programme for auditory processing disorder. All of this learning and training was not only for the benefit of her sons, but from her passion to help others who are struggling on the same journey.

The interventions for her children were chosen on the basis of what would work to help each child improve their status. They were all home-based, non-invasive programs that were highly unlikely to cause any harm. The outcomes didn't always happen quickly – but with perseverance and patience, the results became evident and her boys thrived.

It has been a joy and so encouraging to watch her boys grow and develop into amazing young men over the years that we have known each other. If Jenny had just accepted the initial developmental conclusions she was given, the outcomes that her boys are currently experiencing may have been significantly poorer.

Jenny's passion to share her knowledge and the desire to help other parents has resulted in her writing a number of books. This is the third book in the series, and is focused on the very relevant topic of neurodiversity.

I highly recommend it to you and trust that you will be uplifted, inspired and enlightened by reading it. Having lived with neurodiverse children, Jenny has the experience and insights to help others along the journey.

Glynis Brummer Dip.Teaching, B.Ed, M.Ed (Special Ed), Smart Learning Solutions Limited from NZ.

Julie and Darcy

Just over 18 years ago, we received a pre-natal diagnosis of Down syndrome with our third son, Darcy.

I knew a little about Down syndrome through friendships I had made, which was great because I had a little bit of an understanding of what his needs would look like once he joined our family.

After he was born and we began seeing a paediatrician and attending early intervention, I learned that he was also living with an intellectual disability and was neurodiverse.

I wasn't familiar with this word, but as my son grew I began to understand what it meant. I really loved learning and watching him grow.

He is just like us in so many ways. He is a person, a young man who is now 18 years old and is really thriving with everything he is doing. He loves to socialise, play sport, enjoy a good concert, the theatre and have adventures.

One thing that he does do differently to many others is not worrying about what other people think. We all say that we do this, but I think we do worry at times, especially if it is our friends' opinions.

When we are out, he enjoys every moment of whatever we are doing and does so in a way that everyone can see and enjoy. I often get comments from people wishing they were more like him, so that they could really enjoy the moment.

Darcy has delayed learning in many aspects with speech, fine and gross motor skills, and understanding certain things. However, there are many other things that he completely understands, and a lot of people don't realise this when it comes to people who live with a disability.

He may not be able to express himself like the average person, but he understands everything that people say. He likes people to talk to him directly and ask him questions, rather than through me.

I don't think people mean anything nasty by it, I just think they don't realise that he does understand because he doesn't communicate as clearly as others. He may need assistance from myself or one of his carers, but he will answer questions and talk to others.

He does need assistance with many things such as self-care, communication, writing and reading, but he is also our biggest teacher.

He has taught me that it's okay if something doesn't work the first time – you can try again and again until it does work.

He has taught me real unconditional acceptance of others, and many people could learn a thing or two about this from him. Acceptance and inclusion in the community is so important so that people can live life as it should be lived, and Darcy does this perfectly.

He's taught me to think outside the box so that he can participate in things. I always thought I was good at this, but when Darcy arrived into our family and started growing, I learned new ways to come up with strategies for him.

I love the quirky habits he has and the different way he thinks, and I love the lessons that he teaches us and so many others.

He is the perfect fit to our family and I wouldn't change him for the world. I will, however, change the world for him.

Contents

Foreword	i
Julie and Darcy	iii
Introduction	1
Section 1 - Understanding Neurodiversity	3
What is Neurodiversity?	5
Section 2 - Seven Common Conditions	13
Autism spectrum disorder (ASD)	15
Attention deficit hyperactive disorder (ADHD)	21
Intellectual disability (ID)	25
Dyslexia	29
Dyspraxia	33
Dyscalculia	37
Dysgraphia	41
Story: My Balloon Girl by Sue Dymond	45
Section 3 - Communication strategies	49
Communication strategies	51
Section 4 - Supporting Neurodiversity - (Auditory stimulation)	61
Auditory stimulation (Listening/Sound Therapy)	63
Section 5 - More Inspiring Quotes	71
Albert Einstein – Theoretical physicist	73
Dan Aykroyd – Famous actor	74
Tom Cruise – Hollywood actor	75
Daniel Radcliffe – English actor	76

Leonardo DiCaprio – American actor and film producer 77
Sir Jackie Stewart – F1 driver 78
Michael Phelps – Olympic swimmer 79
Michael Jordan – NBA star 80
Tony Snell – NBA star veteran 81
Heath Shaw – AFL Footballer 82
Katja Dedekind – World's fastest multi-class swimmer 83
Jamie Oliver – Celebrity chef and restauranteur 84
Dylan Alcott – Australian Paralympian, guest speaker & media presenter 85
Sarah Gordy – British actor 86

About the Author 87
Free information seminars 88
Workshop testimonials 91
Acknowledgments 93
References 95

Introduction

This resource follows on from my first book *Building Bright Futures*, and recent publication of pocket book *Educational Moves Reflex Balance and Quick Reference Guide*.

Through writing and publishing *Building Bright Futures* as a neurotherapy toolkit for parents / carers, educators and allied health professionals, I wanted to share my knowledge and research in a book in the area of Neurodiversity for parents, educators and sports coaches. *Understanding Neurodiversity* is a resource for parents / carers, educators and sports coaches to learn more about some of the common labels, along with many tips and ideas for working with individuals in various settings. Throughout the book, there are also many inspiring and positive quotes on neurodiversity.

Over the years, I have worked with many individuals and groups with different diagnoses in helping them to achieve a high level of life skills in their everyday lives. Through my experience I have observed and seen many progressions in an individual's learning, behaviour and motor control, as well as those who are highly skilled on the sporting field through their sports performance advancing to a high level.

The first section, 'Understanding Neurodiversity', gives a snapshot look at seven common neurodiverse conditions. Within this section I have given an overview of some of the common signs and symptoms, their underlying conditions, and some of the special characteristics that individuals may display together with some useful tips and strategies on communication. Following on from this is some helpful information for sports coaches and educators who work with neurodiverse individuals in the classroom and / or sports field through one to one or group settings.

The fourth section goes onto talk about and give a deeper look into the background of Listening Therapy, and how it may support individuals living with a neurodiverse condition.

In the last section, called 'More Inspiring Quotes', there is some enlightening reading on entertainers, athletes and other famous people who live with a neurodiverse condition.

Section 1
Understanding Neurodiversity

What is Neurodiversity?

Neurodiversity is a canopy term that refers to the idea that differences in brain function and behaviour are common, and should be accepted and respected as any other individual variation. It includes a range of differences in individual brain function and behavioural characteristics, often including conditions such as autism, ADHD, dyslexia and others. Being neurodiverse doesn't mean that an individual has low intelligence; sometimes they might be extremely bright and very gifted in certain areas. While everyone has their own cognitive strengths and weaknesses, neurodiversity specifically acknowledges and respects the diverse range of neurological conditions that exist within the human population.

The five quotes depicted below give a wonderful insight into what neurodiversity is and a reminder that everyone has something special to offer.

"Thinking differently is not a disability, it's a strength."
- John Ratey

"My mind may work differently, but it doesn't mean it's broken."
- Stephen Shore

"It's not about 'normal' or 'abnormal', it's about embracing our unique perspectives."
- Judy Singer

"Understanding is the key to acceptance, and acceptance is the path to inclusion."
- Diane Paradiso

"The beauty of neurodiversity is that it challenges our definition of normal."
- Nick Walker

How does the brain process information?

First of all, the brain receives information from our outside world through our five main senses – auditory, visual, tactile, taste and sense of smell.

After the brain gathers specific sensory information, physical messages are sent through the brain's large neurological network. This complex network is comprised of both sensory and motor circuits which are responsible for relaying vital communication around the body on how we think, what we do and how we communicate. Sensory circuits relay information to the brain, whereas the motor circuits will transport information to each muscle within the body. Along with this, there are more complex circuits which are responsible for how we perceive the world around us, controlling both our short and long-term memories, as well as our decision making.

A simple video to watch online which explains how the brain processes information can be found on the website link that is listed in the resources section on page 95.

Learning styles, research and myths

When looking at neurodiversity and how we learn and process information, most of us are very familiar with the common learning styles. These four key styles of learning are generally known as visual, auditory, reading / writing or kinaesthetic learning – some people may know this as 'VARK'.

Visual learners have a strong preference for understanding information through sight – Richard E. Mayer says that "visual learners can communicate complex ideas more effectively than words alone." On the other hand, auditory learners will have a tendency to understand and process things through hearing and listening. Thirdly, having a preference for reading and writing usually means an individual has a preference for reading and taking notes. The fourth style, called kinaesthetic learning, will typically display as an individual having a preference to learning through physical activity.

Research and myths on learning styles

As outlined above, most of us are familiar with what our own learning preference is. Personally, I have a preference to learning new information both visually and kinaesthetically. Interestingly, scientists have tested and researched into this area and have found there is no evidence to suggest these preferences improve an individual's learning.

"Students may have preferences about how to learn, but no evidence suggests that catering to those preferences will lead to better learning."
- Cedar Riener and Daniel Willingham

What researchers found was that the best way to retain information was to make it meaningful – in other words, to organise our thoughts in a certain way. One way to do this was through finding a connection to your own personal situation. Irrespective of how information is presented, researchers found that even if it was duplicated in many different contexts, the outcome was the same. While learning about this, I watched a TEDx video by Tesia Marshik which explored research studies on memory. It is thought that "most of what we learn has meaning". To put it simply, what we learn isn't linked to just one particular sense.

Using multiple senses can be another way to learn and process new information – not only in a classroom or lecture theatre, but also on the sports field. The best way for someone to learn something new is through a multi-sensory approach – kinaesthetic, visual *and* auditory.

1. Being hands on by getting onto the field and experiencing the game physically - kinaesthetic

2. Watching a game of football, or even looking at a drawing on a coach's board showing the different formations / player positions – visual

3. Listening and hearing feedback from coaches and team mates – auditory.

"Incorporating multi-sensory experiences into one lesson makes it more meaningful"
- TEDx Talk video, Learning Styles & the importance of critical self-reflection / Tesia Marshik / TEDxuWLaCrosse

There have been two studies published on whether visual learners remember pictures better. The British Journal of Psychology published a study that assessed the visual and verbal memories of students. Those whose preferred learning style was auditory thought that they would be able to remember words much more easily. Similarly, individuals whose preferred learning style was visual believed that their memory would be better when looking at pictures. Researchers actually found that there was no link between memory and preferred learning styles.

Following on from this, there was a similar study published in the Journal of Educational Psychology. Interestingly, a quote from this publication outlines that Go1 "found no relationship between the study subjects' learning-style preference (visual or auditory) and their performance on reading or listening – comprehension tests. Instead, the visual learners performed best on all kinds of tests."

There have been many studies done within the topic of learning styles, most of them showing that there is no conclusive evidence to suggest that using your preference is the most effective way to learn. Having said this, there is still valid information that says individuals do have different preferences. In an article by Educational Next, 'The Stubborn Myth of "Learning Styles", they state that "different types of information are processed in different parts of the brain. It is also true that individuals have differences in abilities and preferences."

It is important to note that having a preferred learning style is not the same as having a learning difficulty. Someone who is neurodiverse may not learn in the best way if they just focus on how they prefer to learn. Offering different mediums through a multi-sensory approach can be just as effective. Learning styles and preferences are just one effective learning tool.

> *"There is no "good and bad" learning – there is only effective and not effective learning"*
> **- Kamran Ayub, Dec 1, 2022.**

When it comes to understanding diagnostic labels / neurodiverse conditions, no two individuals are the same. Some conditions may solely stand alone and others may overlap with one another. Seven of the most common labels are outlined and described below: autism spectrum disorder (ASD), attention deficit hyperactive disorder (ADHD), intellectual disability, dyslexia, dyspraxia, dyscalculia and dysgraphia.

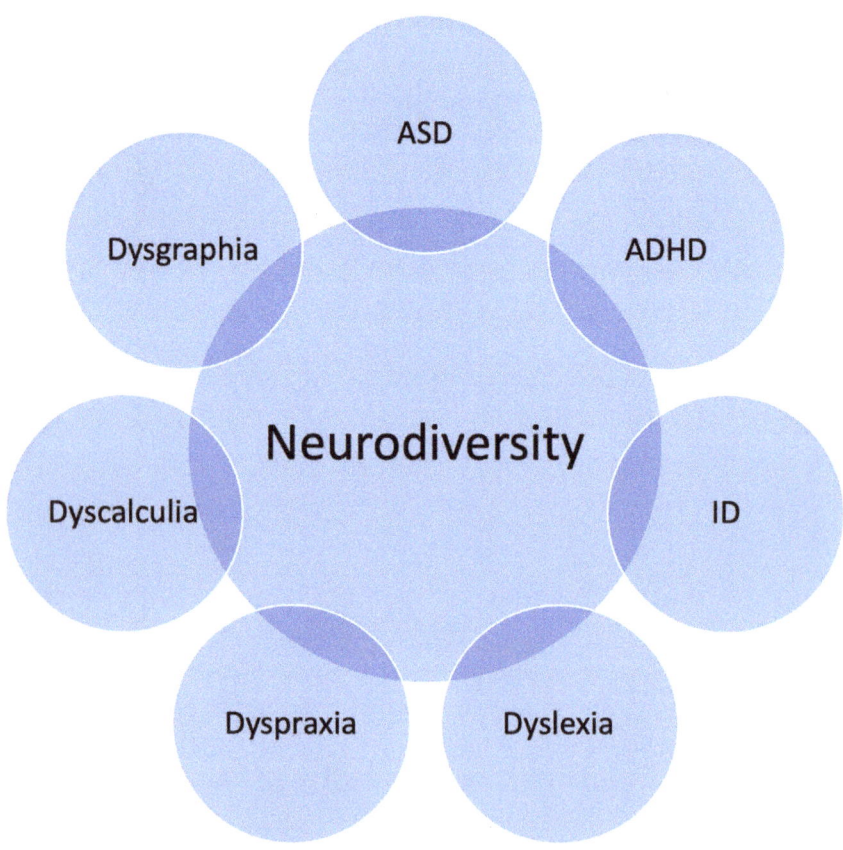

"Neurodiversity is reminder that we all have something unique to offer, and that makes the world more interesting."
- Nick Walker

These seven common neurodiverse conditions are described in more detail in section two.

Tables one and two below show a more detailed picture of the many neurodiverse conditions.

Table one	Table two
• Autism spectrum disorder (ASD) • Attention deficit hyperative disorder (ADHD) • Intellectual disability (ID) • Dyslexia • Dyspraxia • Dyscalculia • Dysgraphia	• Tourette syndrome (TS) • Oppositional defiant disorder (ODD) • Gifted • Sensory integration disorder • Auditory processing disorder • Anxiety • Specific learning disorders • Trauma and mental health • Down syndrome • Obsessive compulsive disorder

"We don't need to be fixed, we need to be understood."
- John Elder Robinson

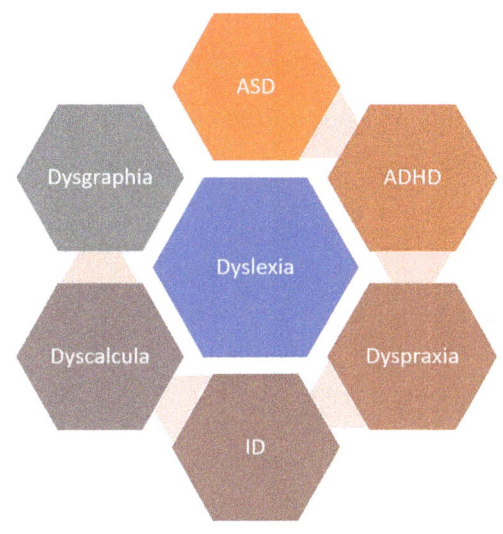

Section 2
Seven Common Conditions

Autism spectrum disorder (ASD)

What is ASD?

Autism spectrum disorder (ASD) is a lifelong condition that is both neurological and developmental. It is typically diagnosed in early childhood, often by the age of two. Some of the common characteristics can present as:

◊ **limited interests and repetitive behaviours**
◊ **challenges with communication and social interaction.**

It is a condition that is four times more likely to be diagnosed in males than females, primarily affecting how people communicate, learn and behave. Many have difficulty with their communication but others can have a high level of speech and language centred around a certain topic which they can explain in great detail. A diagnosis of ASD needs to be done through a registered health professional and due to it being a 'spectrum', it can range from mild through to severe.

What causes ASD? Many researchers aren't fully sure of the primary causes of ASD. It is thought through research and findings that an individual's genetic pre disposition and environment may contribute to a delay in their development, leading to ASD. Some increased risks on developing ASD could be:

◊ **sibling with ASD**
◊ **being born to older parents**

- **experiencing difficult birth, very low birth weight**
- **genetic and chromosomal conditions, such as Fragile X syndrome or Down syndrome.**

Children who are diagnosed with ASD will often show some of the following communication and behavioural challenges, and display some restrictive and repetitive behaviours. Some individuals may go through their childhood and teenage years without a diagnosis of Autism until they reach adulthood. This can be the case if an adult person gathers and reads information about ASD and then chooses to seek out advice from a health professional.

Common signs & symptoms of ASD

- **non-verbal communication challenges**
    * poor eye contact
    * hand gestures
    * facial expressions and emotions
    * become frustrated – difficulty communicating their thoughts

- **repetitive behaviours**
    * rocking and flapping
    * squealing
    * clearing the throat
    * switching lights on and off

- **limited imaginative play and narrow interests**
    * playing with cars
    * trains
    * dolls
    * collecting sticks or leaves
    * have other specific hobbies and interests

- **may be an expert in their professional field of work**
- **thrives on routines**
    * may become upset if routines are suddenly changed

- ◊ may display a monotone voice when talking
- ◊ may repeat words / phrases (called echolalia)
- ◊ may show signs of poor listening when others are speaking to them
- ◊ have difficulty with communication
    * slow development and or low level of language skills
- ◊ have trouble understanding what is said to them in a social situation
- ◊ sleep difficulties and irritability / bad temper
- ◊ sensitive or oversensitive to clothing, temperature, light and sound.

"My whole thing is to entertain, make people laugh and to forget about the real world for a little while."
- Dan Akroyd

Special characteristics of ASD

May be very artistic

Talented with music

May be exceptional with maths and science

Sport

Good with mechanics

Exceptional memory skills

"Kids have to be exposed to different things in order to develop. A child's not going to find out he likes to play a musical instrument if you never exposed him to it…"
- Temple Grandin

Underlying conditions with ASD

"You're off to great places! Today is your day! Your mountain is waiting, so get on your way!"
- Dr Seuss

On the whole, individuals living with a diagnosis of ASD may be strong learners and remember information which is quite detailed. They may be highly intelligent in the areas of mathematics, science, or within the creative arts – music, drama, art and dance. When looking at the sensory system, an individual with ASD may be a highly visual learner, or the opposite – where they learn better through their auditory system. Whether you are working with a child or adult in a learning or sports coaching capacity, it is important to remember that no two individuals are the same.

> *"Today you are you! That is truer than true!*
> *There is no one alive that is you-er than you!"*
> **- Dr Seuss**

Attention deficit hyperactive disorder (ADHD)

What is ADHD?

Attention-deficit hyperactivity disorder (ADHD) is a neurological condition that is one of the most common disorders diagnosed in childhood – though it also often persists into adulthood. It is characterised by frequent and various forms of inattention, impulsive behaviours, and hyperactivity. ADHD can present in three primary ways at the time of diagnosis:

- **predominantly inattentive presentation: difficulty sustaining attention, easily distracted, and poor concentration**
- **predominantly hyperactive-impulsive presentation: excessive fidgeting, inability to sit still, and impulsive actions**
- **combined presentation: features of both inattentiveness and hyperactivity-impulsivity.**

Common symptoms of ADHD

- **trouble sitting still – constantly fidgeting / squirming**
- **needing to constantly move their body and move around**
- **easily distracted**
- **poor attention and concentration when**

- * playing with toys or
- * doing schoolwork

◊ **may interrupt others unnecessarily, and participate in activities quite loudly**

◊ **poor planning and difficulty with time management**
- * difficulty keeping track of time and / or sticking to a schedule

◊ **may change jobs frequently**
- * sensitive to criticism
- * low job performance due to nature of disorganisation and being impulsive

◊ **constantly fidgeting, can't sit still**

◊ **easily distracted and difficultly sitting still**
- * while watching a movie or TV show, or when trying to concentrate on a work task

◊ **always feeling the need to be busy**

◊ **very emotionally sensitive**

◊ **poor financial planning skills – often spending money impulsively.**

"I have OCD mixed with ADD, you try living with that. It's complicated."
- Justin Timberlake

"I'm a perfectionist. I can't help it. I get really upset with myself if I fail in the least."
- Justin Timberlake

Special characteristics of ADHD

Very creative

Ability to hyperfocus when working on a particular task

Great problem solver

High levels of resilience

Excel at sport, due to high energy levels

High achievers in their field, i.e. business, research, invention, performing arts

"Why fit in when you were born to stand out?"
- Dr. Suess

Underlying conditions with ADHD

- Heath Shaw

Intellectual disability (ID)

What is intellectual disability?

Children and adults diagnosed with Intellectual disability (ID) can vary widely from person to person. This diagnosis is lifelong and is usually diagnosed when an individual is learning and developing slower and below their expected developmental milestones – i.e. learning to talk, fine and gross motor skills, through to learning at school.

It can occur before birth, at any time during a child's development, or right through to adulthood. Intellectual disability before birth is most commonly caused by Down syndrome, genetic conditions, Fragile X syndrome, fetal alcohol syndrome, and infections. Sometimes the cause of a person's Intellectual disability may occur during birth or soon after. Other causes of Intellectual disability may not happen until later on in a child's life and may be caused through an infection, stroke or a severe head injury.

Common symptoms of intellectual disability

- ◊ **may have delayed language / learn to talk later**
- ◊ **difficulty remembering things**
- ◊ **difficulty talking with others**
- ◊ **delay in meeting fine and gross motor milestones during childhood development. Slower when learning to:**
    - * roll over
    - * sit
    - * crawl and / or walk
- ◊ **difficulty problem solving and understanding social**

situations
- challenges with learning at school
- IQ tests will be lower than the standard scores
- difficulty understanding social cues and controlling emotions
- may find reading, writing and communicating with others challenging
- may take things literally due to lack of understanding
- difficulty processing information, thinking logically and solving problems
- relies heavily upon nonverbal communication – eye contact, tone of voice, body language.

"Doesn't matter who you are; we are all just human beings."
- Sarah Gordy

Special characteristics of intellectual disability

Enjoy areas of creative arts

Usually very truthful

Strong appreciation for things of beauty

Love learning, even though it may be challenging

Strong discipline

Value honesty and fairness

"I don't have a disability, I have a different-ability."
- Robert M. Hensel

Underlying conditions with intellectual disability (ID)

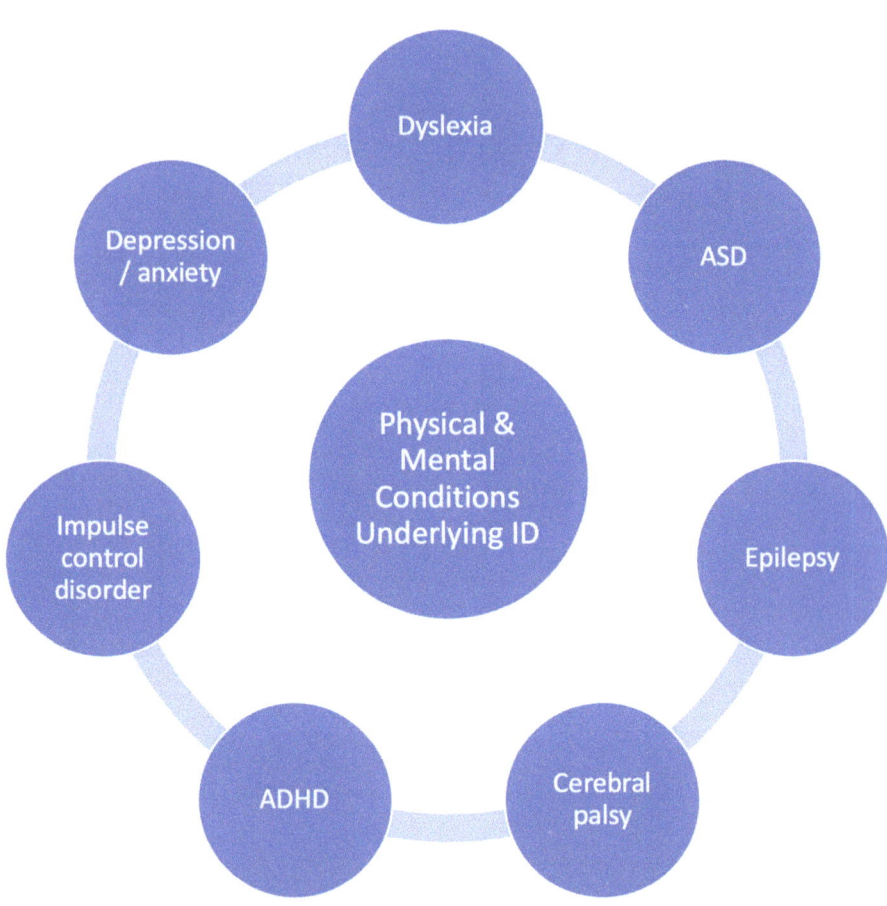

"I have a disability yes that's true, but all that really means is I may have to take a slightly different path than you."
- Robert M. Hensel

Dyslexia

What is dyslexia?

Dyslexia is a specific learning disability that affects a person's ability to read and spell. Someone diagnosed with this condition will most likely have difficulty with understanding language and associations around words. A diagnosis of dyslexia has no reflection on an individual's intelligence.

The cause of dyslexia may rely on a few different situations. The main reason is genetics – if a family member or parent has dyslexia, then there is about a 30%-50% chance of developing the condition. Dyslexia may also be evident in those with Down syndrome. The second area in which dyslexia may develop is through how the brain develops through its structure, chemistry and function. Thirdly, in utero, a foetus may have been exposed to an infection, toxin or other factors which may disrupt how the brain develops.

Common symptoms of dyslexia

- ◊ **speech delay**
- ◊ **difficulties with articulation**
- ◊ **may have trouble learning rhymes, colours and shapes**
- ◊ **adverse to reading books – usually reads below expected age level**

- ◊ **often writes words backwards – i.e. may write the word 'tap' when the actual word should have been 'pat'**
- ◊ **confusion between the sounds and shapes of letters – i.e. 'p', 'd', 'b', 'q' and 'm' and 'w'**
- ◊ **challenges with reading, and / or spelling**
- ◊ **may avoid writing**
- ◊ **challenges with reading**
- ◊ **may confuse left and right**
- ◊ **difficulty with concentration, staying focussed when listening to a conversation**
- ◊ **poor time management and organisational skills – finds it difficult to prioritise tasks**
- ◊ **may avoid particular types of study and work**
- ◊ **may need the support of someone else to read documents / emails.**

"Being dyslexic, I had to train myself to focus my attention. I became very visual and learned how to create mental images in order to comprehend what I read."
- Tom Cruise

Special characteristics of dyslexia

Great drawing skills

May excel at sport

Very observant

Highly empathetic

'Big picture' thinkers

Strong memory skills

"Being diagnosed with dyslexia at age 60 was like the last part of the puzzle in a tremendous mystery that I've kept to myself for all these years."
- Stephen Spielberg

Underlying conditions with dyslexia

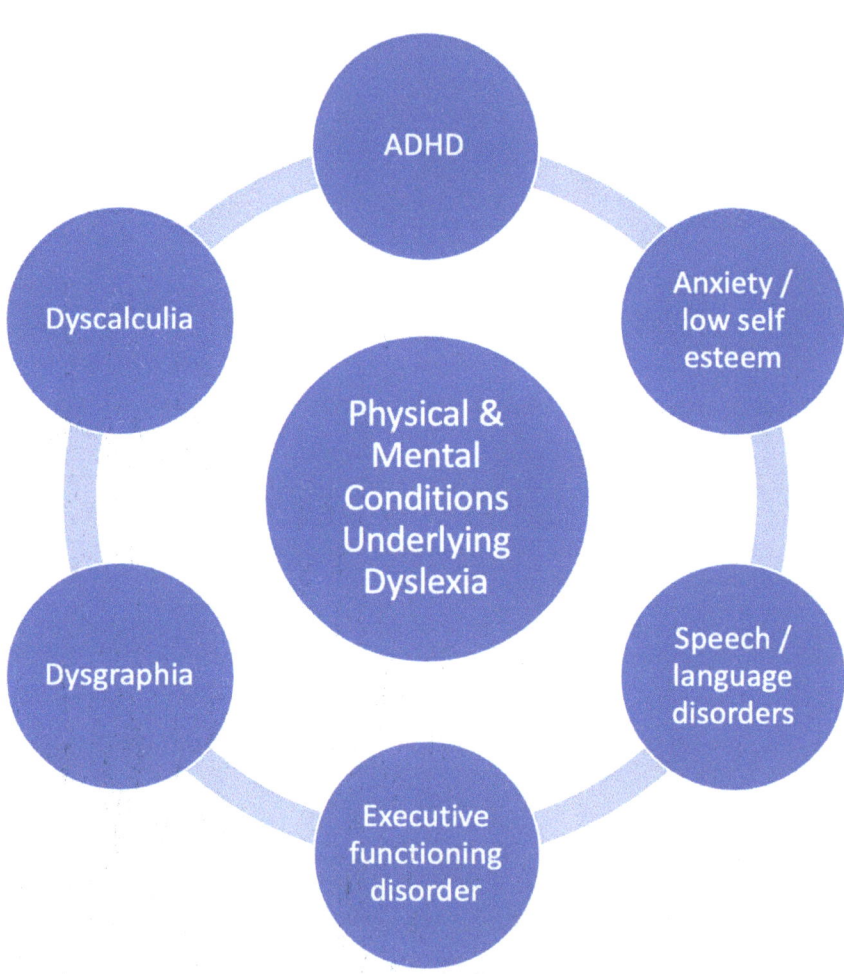

"I am not disabled by dyslexia, I am empowered by it."
- Jamie Oliver

Dyspraxia

What is dyspraxia?

Dyspraxia is a condition that affects a person's movement and coordination. It is commonly picked up in children very early on in their development. It may also occur in adults after an acquired brain injury, stroke, severe illness or as a symptom of dementia.

There are three types of dyspraxia – motor, verbal, and oral. Motor dyspraxia is seen in individuals who have difficulties with motor coordination – i.e. hopping, skipping, kicking / throwing a ball, dressing, and even writing. On the other hand, verbal dyspraxia relates to people who have challenges with coordinating speech sounds and fluency. Lastly, oral dyspraxia relates to an individual who has poor muscle coordination within their mouth and tongue muscles – i.e. difficulty swallowing and eating food / drinks.

Common symptoms of dyspraxia

- ◊ **messy eating**
- ◊ **awkward and clumsy movements**
- ◊ **accident-prone**
- ◊ **poor spatial awareness – crashing / bumping in to objects or people**
- ◊ **difficulty with fine and gross motor skills – i.e. writing / drawing, speech, doing up buttons on a shirt, jumping and / or running**

- ◊ may have a narrow range of language – i.e. limited vocabulary
- ◊ may appear to speak more slowly than their peers
- ◊ underachievement at school, due to challenges with hand writing and speech
- ◊ poor balance and coordination, and may tire easily
- ◊ poor organisational skills at work or uni / TAFE study
- ◊ may have trouble with everyday tasks, such as preparing meals and dressing
- ◊ poor time management and planning
- ◊ difficulty remembering new information
- ◊ may have difficulties with social and emotional situations as well as performing everyday motor tasks.

"It has never held me back. Some of the smartest people I know are people who have learning disabilities."
- Daniel Radcliffe

Special characteristics of dyspraxia

Highly empathetic

Very creative

Strategic thinkers

Good problem solvers

Excellent listeners

"You have brains in your head. You have feet in your shoes. You can steer yourself any direction you choose."
- Dr. Seuss

Underlying conditions with dyspraxia

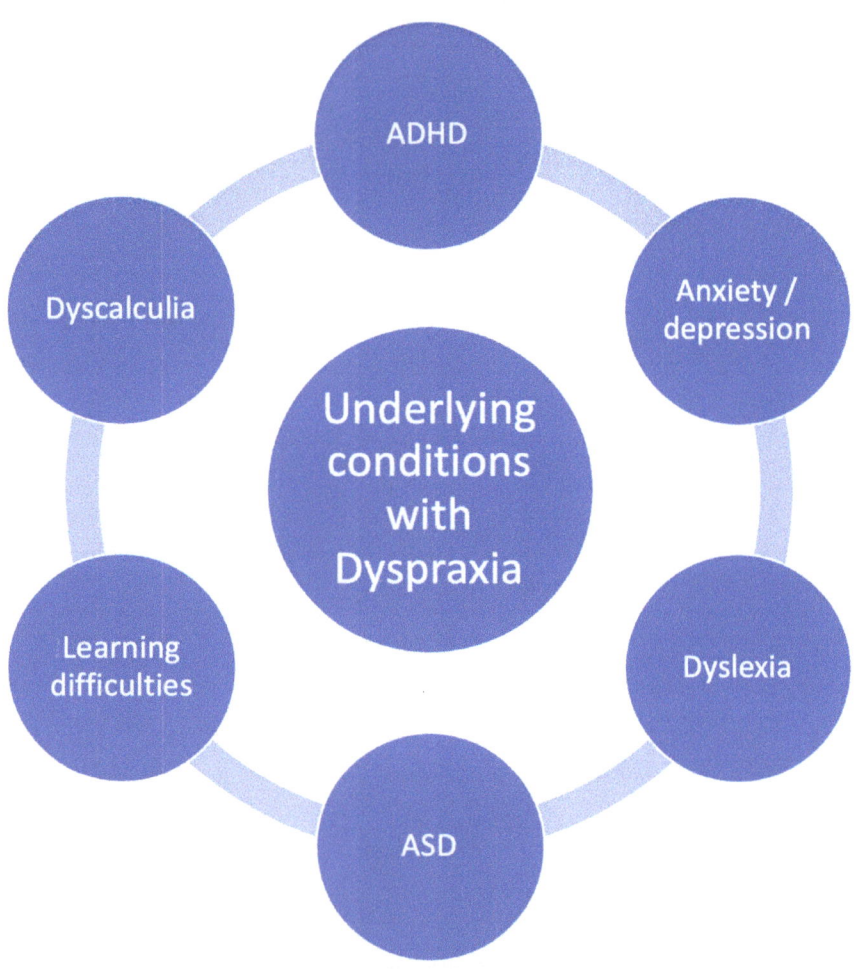

"I'm not clumsy, I'm just accident-prone."
- Daniel Radcliffe

Dyscalculia

What is dyscalculia?

Dyscalculia is a specific learning disorder that can be seen in a person who has difficulty doing mathematical skills. It is often hereditary, and is quite commonly diagnosed very early in primary school, but may show up during the teenage or young adult years. Even though it may run in families, there is still a lot more research needed in this area to fully understand its onset.

Those diagnosed with dyscalculia may also have another neurodiverse condition, such as ASD, ADHD, dyslexia, or dyspraxia.

Common symptoms of dyscalculia

- ◊ **difficulty reading a clock face and knowing what the time is**
- ◊ **have trouble remembering things that have numbers, i.e:**
    * phone numbers
    * postcodes
    * sporting game scores
- ◊ **difficulty with directions – knowing which way is left and which way is right**
- ◊ **below grade level for maths at school**
- ◊ **preference for counting on fingers beyond lower primary school**

- ◊ **delayed in basic maths, i.e:**
  - * addition
  - * subtraction
  - * learning & remembering times tables
  - * division
- ◊ **may have poor understanding of numerical and word connections, i.e. numerical symbol and corresponding word – '8', and 'eight'.**

"It is only with the heart that one can see clearly, for the most essential things are invisible to the eye."
– **Hans Christian Andersen**

Special characteristics of dyscalculia

Great problem solvers

Very creative - artistic, imaginative

Strategic thinkers

Intuitive thinkers

Often good at reading, writing, and spelling

Often very good with their hands

Cher wrote in her autobiography, *The First Time* -
"I couldn't read quickly enough to get all my homework done and, for me, math was like trying to understand Sanskrit. Almost everything I learned, I had to learn by listening. My report cards always said I was not living up to my potential."
- Cher

Underlying conditions with dyscalculia

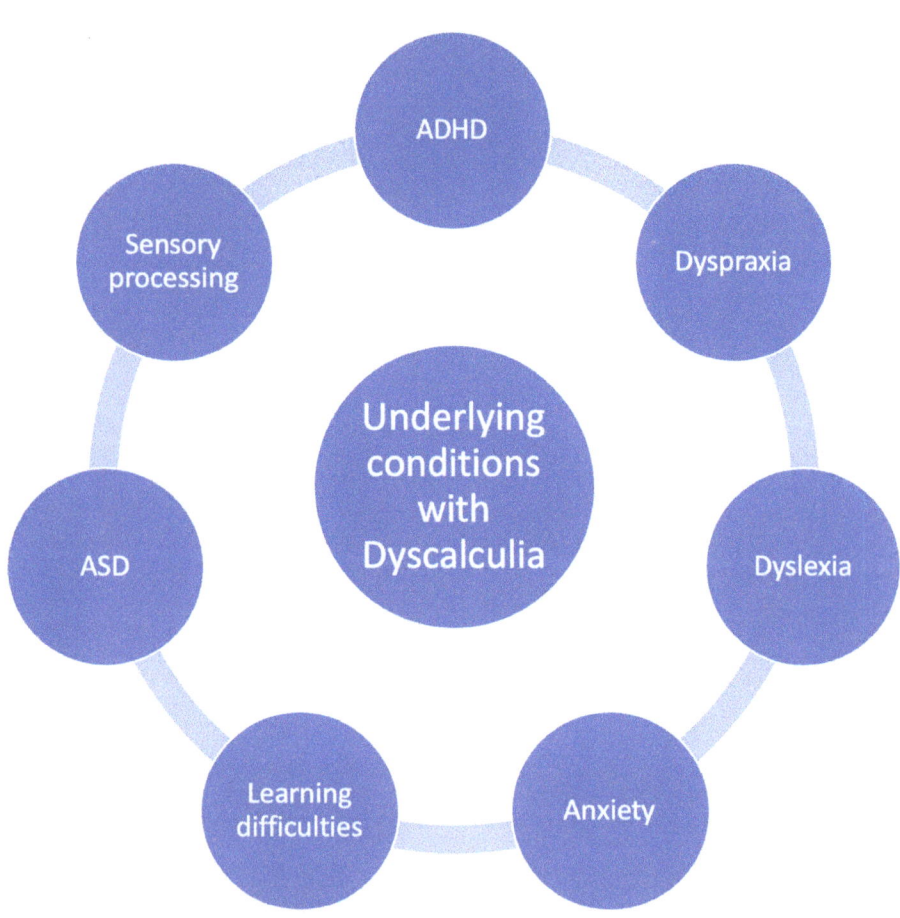

"I didn't fail the test, I just found 100 ways to do it wrong."
– **Benjamin Franklin**

Dysgraphia

What is dysgraphia?

Children and adults diagnosed with dysgraphia learn differently due to their challenges with writing and being able to put their thoughts down on paper. It is thought that dysgraphia is genetic, however its exact genetic basis is not fully understood. It is often picked up early on in children who have difficulty mastering the skill of writing. Writing skills in children typically happen around six years of age.

Common symptoms of dysgraphia

- **difficulty copying words onto paper**
- **slow writing skills**
- **poor fine motor coordination**
- **poor concentration when having to write**
- **letters may appear in different styles and incorrectly spaced**
- **may leave words out when writing sentences**
- **difficulty understanding the correct use of verbs and pronouns in sentences and paragraphs**
- **challenges with holding a pen or pencil currently**
- **letters and words on a page may be difficult to read – they may appear in different sizes and have uneven spacing**

Special characteristics of dysgraphia

Strong memory through verbal information

Strong leadership skills

Often very imaginative at finding alternative ways to solve problems

Strong expressive language skills

Often very good at seeing the bigger picture in something

"Just writing and being in the studio was like therapy for me."
- Justin Timberlake

Underlying conditions with dysgraphia

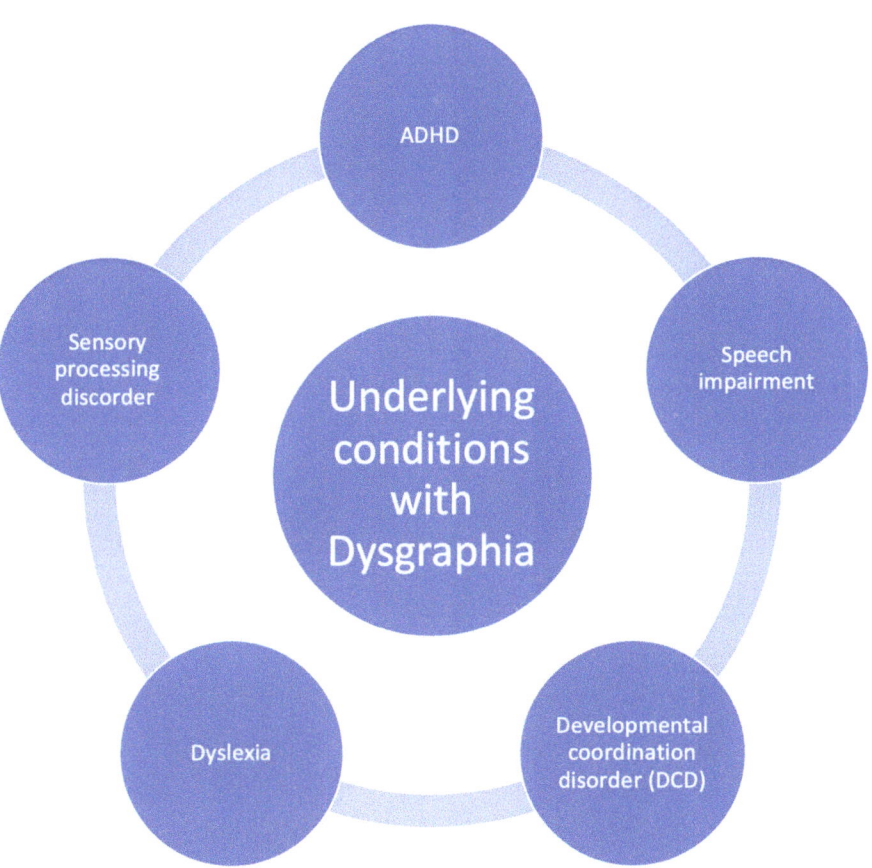

"It's not our disabilities, it's our abilities that count"
- Chris Burke

My Balloon Girl
By: Sue Dymond

Forty-three years ago, my beautiful daughter was born.

I was a young, teen-aged mum and had no idea about life – never mind parenting.

Shannon was a very challenging baby but as she developed into a toddler and young girl, she became delightful.

Before she was toilet trained, I bundled her into a Kombi van and went travelling around Australia, eventually settling in Melbourne, Victoria.

In primary school, Shan became very fussy with her food. I didn't think much of it, as she was allergic to dairy products, and I saw this as a phase.

The phase did not fade and her food options became more and more limited. As a mum who also worked fulltime, I had no time to cook multiple meals, so it was eat what I make, or make it yourself. As a 12-year-old, she did just that, started making her own meals.

I took her to the doctor as I was concerned she was not getting a good balance of food. He asked if she runs around a lot or if she is always tired. Shan was always active. His words were: "she is getting what she needs, so don't worry". Those 8 words changed our worlds – I stopped worrying and we stopped fighting!

Shan was not interested in school work but, because she was very popular, she loved going to school. She just day dreamed through twelve years of classes. This was a huge concern for me – what will happen to her when she leaves school…

What happened was, she did some very ugly jobs, left those jobs and eventually fell into jobs she has an interest in.

I have another daughter (Chloe). She is ten years younger than Shannon and has Down syndrome.

Chloe and I always refer to Shan as the balloon girl. Shan always has a million thoughts going through her head at one time and is trying to action each and every one of these thoughts!

On the other hand Chloe and I are very grounded, Shan is always floating around with her thoughts and we have to grab the balloon strings to pull her back down to the ground.

When Shan finds something she is passionate about, she is very one tracked. The conversations are always around her passions (roller skating and travel now).

I have learnt over the years to just be rude and stop her mid-sentence, then completely change the subject.

When Shan was 40 years old she was diagnosed with ADHD. She said this diagnosis has given her a reason for her ways.

I was not at all surprised as I have been working in the disability sector for many years now and had assumed this was the case.

I jokingly said to her when she told me:

"Aren't you glad I didn't know that when you were young, I may have tried to protect you from life!"

Her response was: **"Oh Ma, I am so grateful you didn't know, I learnt to be resilient, flexible and how to not let my anxiety and ADHD become the focus of my life"**.

Shannon is perfect, just as she is, and she is our balloon girl!

Section 3
Communication Strategies

Communication strategies

After reading and understanding about the seven most common neurodiverse conditions, you will have noticed that strengths and weaknesses can vary from person to person – but may also overlap. For example, an individual on the autism spectrum might have strong reading skills and poor expressive language. On the other hand, another individual with ASD might have very strong and detailed verbal skills, but struggle with reading and writing. An athlete with dyslexia will learn plays and positions much easier through visual cues – e.g. drawing plays up on a coach's board, even walking through a play physically one-to-one. Some communication strategies to consider when working with neurodiverse individuals at home, in the classroom, or sporting field are to:

◊ **use eye contact and speak at their level**

◊ **use their special interest to engage learning and understanding**

◊ **try not to use jokes**

◊ **use lots of visual cues – pictures / diagrams can be very beneficial**

◊ **use closed questions when asking something to a student – e.g. 'Do you like ice-cream or chocolate?' 'Are you feeling better today?'**

These five communication strategies above, together with the ones listed for each of the seven common neurodiverse conditions, can be applied to all neurodiverse individuals across many different settings – education, sports training / coaching, and even at home.

> *"The old Nürburgring had 187 corners per lap, and I can still give you every gear change, every braking distance on each of the 187 corners. But I can't say the alphabet."*
> **- Sir Jackie Stewart**

Autism spectrum disorder (ASD)

Use social stories

Use visual aids

Allow plenty of time for processing information

Avoid using non-verbal communication - i.e. body language, gestures, facial expressions

Avoid asking too many questions

Speak slowly and clearly - use very few words

Find their special interest - choose an engaging activity

Use eye contact, and speak at their level

"If they can't learn the way we teach, we teach the way they learn."
- Dr. O. Ivar Lovaas

Attention deficit hyperactive disorder (ADHD)

Try to avoid making statements – use questions instead

Try to give specific directions when setting a task

Speak in a clear voice and offer choices

Find a quiet space free from distractions

Use eye contact when talking

Remove technology out of sight – less distracting

Break up tasks – try & finish one thing before moving onto the next

Include movement activities - fun bean bag exercises, jumping on a trampoline, go for a run or walk

"I haven't failed. I've just found 10,000 ways to that won't work."
- Thomas Edison

Intellectual disability (ID)

Speak slowly and communicate at their level

Use picture cards

Use a communication book

Find the appropriate communication style, i.e. sign language, visual cues, written text, communication devices

Be patient and enthusiastic when talking or playing

Look beyond their capabilities

Use eye contact

"It takes an open minded individual to look beyond a disability, and see that ability has so much more to offer than the limitations society tries to place upon them."
- Robert M. Hensel

Dyslexia

Be patient and calm

Use larger fonts in written work, emails, or text messages

Use visual cues rather than verbal instructions

Listen attentively

Use different colours / highlights – grouping similar information together

Use lip movements and facial expressions to assist with understanding language

Use voice messages

Draw a picture on a coaching board, print off copies of new plays, use flashcards

"Being dyslexic is actually an advantage and has helped me greatly in life. I see my condition as a gift."
- Sir Richard Branson

Dyspraxia

Allow plenty of time for processing verbal instructions

Try to create a calm and relaxed environment

Use gestures, visual and written language

Be patient and offer lots of reassurance

Regularly use specific exercises given by their speech pathologist

Ask questions that require a YES / NO answer

Try to limit distractions

Learn how to touch type if handwriting is challenging

"Working hard is important. But there is something that matters even more, believing in yourself."
- Daniel Radcliffe

Dysgraphia

Learn to touch type, due to challenges with hand writing

Use text to speech technology / software

Spell words out a loud, rather than writing them down

Try using thicker pens / pencils and pencil grips for more comfort when writing

Try using lined paper that has wider lines - even coloured paper

Allow students to bring a device to record a lecture

Try different hand exercises - squeeze a stress ball, shake the hands, rotate the wrists, finger and thumb exercises

Be patient and allow plenty of time for an individual to process their thoughts and ideas

"Each impossible mission can be made possible if you put your mind to it and work hard without giving up." - **Sujeet Desai**

Dyscalculia

Break up complex maths problems into individual subsets

Use visual and verbal cues

Talk and write down maths equations in words

Try to use short and frequent study sessions

Be patient, and offer lots of encouragement

Allow extra time for solving maths problems

Create visual reference cards to help revise and learn maths problems

Try putting the maths equation into a picture

"Software is a great combination between artistry and engineering."
- Bill Gates

Section 4
*Supporting Neurodiversity
(Auditory Stimulation)*

Auditory stimulation (Listening / Sound Therapy)

Background on auditory stimulation

Auditory stimulation can also be known as 'listening therapy' or 'sound therapy'. The area of sound therapy was first pioneered in the late 1940s by Dr. Alfred Tomatis. Dr. Tomatis was a French ear, nose and throat specialist who discovered through his research that he could repair the damaged hearing of opera singers and factory workers. This was done by playing to them the sounds that they could no longer hear, and as a result he discovered the link between the ear and the voice.

Through his research and learnings, Dr. Tomatis therefore found that by improving the way we listen it could dramatically improve our learning, balance, coordination, and posture – as well as communication and creativity. He found that both adults and children experienced improved attention, memory and focus. Those who displayed specific learning issues saw a lessening of their difficulties. Dr. Tomatis therefore realised that **listening problems** are the baseline cause of many learning problems, and he went on to develop a highly effective technique to fix them. His work laid the foundation for understanding the importance of auditory processing and its impact on various aspects of human functioning, including learning and communication.

> *"The sensory apparatus we know as the ear is simply an external attribute of the cerebral cortex."*
> **- Dr. Alfred Tomatis**

What can sound therapy or listening therapy do?

The different frequency of sounds exercise the ear, which then helps the brain to better focus on sounds by filtering out those that are not needed. It uses specially recorded classical music and nature sounds to help people process sound better and improve their listening.

Ear infections, tonsillitis and allergies are common in young children, and as a result can affect a child's ability to hear certain frequencies – thus affecting their auditory processing ability. Sound therapy may help restore the ability to hear certain frequencies, which ultimately has the capacity for individuals to improve their focus, concentration, learning, communication, motor and behavioural challenges.

Frequency of sounds

Through Dr. Tomatis's research, he also learnt that there seemed to be a connection between particular sound frequencies. These different sound frequencies appeared to have a positive impact on improving the body and mind. When doing auditory stimulation, the different frequencies of sounds target different areas of the neurological sensory system. The frequency chart that Dr. Tomatis identified were categorised into the following three zones:

Zone 1 – *Lower frequency sounds (sensory integration)*

This zone works on enhancing:

- ◊ body awareness

- ◊ posture
- ◊ muscle tone
- ◊ balance and coordination
- ◊ rhythm
- ◊ discrimination of left / right
- ◊ laterality and sense of direction.

Zone 2 – *Mid to High frequency sounds (speech and language)*

This zone aims to work on improving:

- ◊ focus and concentration
- ◊ attention
- ◊ memory
- ◊ expressive and receptive language
- ◊ spelling
- ◊ maths
- ◊ vocal control.

Zone 3 – *Higher frequency sounds (high spectrum)*

This zone aims to work on further developing:

- ◊ improved energy
- ◊ auditory cohesion
- ◊ self-confidence
- ◊ ideas
- ◊ ideals
- ◊ intuition – better perception
- ◊ emotional regulation.

Listening and Hearing

Are listening and hearing the same?

No, they are completely different!

Many people can have normal hearing, but experience listening difficulties without even knowing it.

Listening: listening is a very active process and is shaped very early from about 18 weeks in utero. We therefore develop our own set of neural pathways to listen from, as early as conception. Listening is what we do with the sounds our ears collect.

Hearing: hearing is extremely passive, and is the process by which we collect sound.

The most important sense in children for their learning is ***hearing***. For example, if you compare deaf children with blind children, by grade four a deaf child will be approximately two years behind a blind child. However, it is ***listening*** that helps to define our life performance.

Benefits of Sound Therapy

The benefits of sound therapy are enormous, and can help an individual in so many different ways. It can assist with overcoming learning difficulties associated with neurodevelopmental conditions such as ADHD, autism, learning delay, dyslexia, dyspraxia and many others. It may help to improve concentration, memory, attention, communication, written language, motor development, posture, balance, co-ordination, public speaking, stuttering and poor vocabulary. At the same time, sound therapy can also reduce anxiety, fatigue, help with emotional regulation, and increase energy.

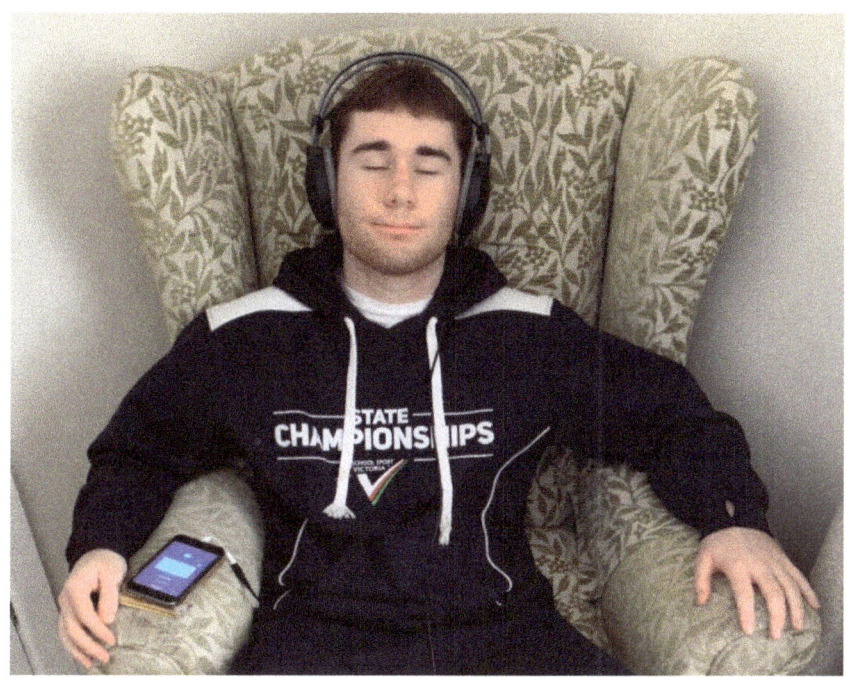

Three listening therapies which I have completed training in, as well as having personal experience with my own family and clients, are Johansen Individualised Auditory Stimulation (JIAS), Integrated Listening Systems (iLs) and The Listening Program (TLP). These listening therapies can be read in more detail in my first book *Building Bright Futures*.

One which I like to recommend with helping to improve difficulties associated with neurodiverse conditions is Johansen Individualised Auditory Stimulation (JIAS).

What is JIAS?

Johansen Individualised Auditory Stimulation (also known as Johansen Sound Therapy) was developed in Denmark by Dr. Kjeld Johansen, Director of the Baltic Dyslexic Research Laboratory, from the original work by Christian A. Volf.

It was developed to stimulate the nerve pathways into and within the brain. JIAS is specifically directed to the pathways between the right ear and the left hemisphere of the brain, where information from the ears is first received, and then moves down to the deeper processing areas.

Who can benefit?

Children, adolescents and adults can benefit from the JIAS program. For older individuals, the program may take longer to complete than it would for younger people. Through a consistent approach to the program, individuals can enjoy 'better listening' which can show improvements in:

◊ reading
◊ spelling
◊ learning
◊ handling with background noise
◊ enhanced social skills
◊ learning new words
◊ remembering what you hear
◊ better listening and attention
◊ focus and concentration
◊ following instructions
◊ being able to sing in tune
◊ social skills.

Treatment and reviews

An initial listening assessment is done through an audiogram, which tests the left and right ear dominance. The audiogram is able to show an individual's listening ability and how their left and right ears are tracking according the optimal listening curve. This process usually takes an hour to complete.

From this audiogram, the client is then given a specially recorded set of music to listen to for 10 minutes a day, six days a week. The average length of the program is approximately nine to ten months.

The music is unique to the client, and is downloaded onto a device which is listened to through over-ear headphones that have a specific left and right ear. After the required listening phase, 45-minute reviews are conducted where a new listening test is performed. If any changes appear on the audiogram, new music is made up and then listened to for the next phase.

If an individual is under seven years of age, or is unable to sit through a listening test, there is a generic program which can be offered. The generic program lasts 20 weeks, and consists of a set of five music files that are listened to for four weeks.

Auditory stimulation can have many benefits for neurodiverse individuals, helping them to function better in their world. These can be advantageous in helping them to thrive in one of their special talents, be better able to follow instructions in a noisy environment, improve one's self-esteem, learn better in the classroom, be less anxious, and have improved focus and concentration.

Research in JIAS

On the Johansen IAS website, there are five articles to read to gain a further insight into some of the positive results through a range of research – including single case, large scale, and matched group studies.

The five research papers all give a comprehensive understanding of the benefits into JIAS. The link to these research papers can be found in the resources section on page 102. These papers are:

- ◊ A Retrospective Study at the Sensomotoric Centre in Mjolby, Sweden
- ◊ A Two-Year Evaluation Project in East Lothian and Midlothian, Scotland
- ◊ A Single Case-Study in Helsinki, Finland
- ◊ A Four-Year Implementation Study in Minneapolis, USA
- ◊ A Study on Dyslexic Students in Holland.

In my book *Building Bright Futures*, there are several case studies that can be read within the section titled 'Stories and Testimonials'. Along with JIAS case studies, there are stories of individuals who have improved their neurodiverse condition through developmental movement programs.

Section 5

More Inspiring Quotes

(Celebrities, athletes & other famous people)

Albert Einstein

Theoretical physicist

Albert Einstein is extremely well known for being a genius in maths and science. Growing up, he had some learning challenges with spelling and grammar, writing his thoughts down on paper and other fine motor tasks such as tying his shoelaces.

Through all his challenges, Einstein became famous for his theory of relativity, and he also ended up winning a Nobel Prize for his quantum theory.

"Once we accept our limits, we go beyond them."

"It's not that I'm so smart, it's just that I stay with problems longer."

"Logic will get you from A to B. Imagination will take you everywhere."

Dan Aykroyd

Famous actor

Dan Akroyd is a famous Canadian-born actor and is well known for his part in the movie *Ghostbusters*. Interestingly, two of his obsessions were with ghosts and law enforcement. In particular, he loved to carry a police badge around with him. The movie *Ghostbusters* came about through his obsessions, and in particular, one of the greatest ghost hunters, Hans Holzer.

"You look at the floor and see the floor. I look at the floor and see molecules."

"I do not suffer from Asperger's syndrome; I embrace it"

"One of my symptoms included my obsession with ghosts and law enforcement - I carry around a police badge with me, for example. I became obsessed by Hans Holzer, the greatest ghost hunter ever. That's when the idea of my film 'Ghostbusters' was born."

Tom Cruise

Hollywood actor

Tom Cruise's difficulties with reading were very challenging for him, as he would struggle with remembering what he had just read. This caused him to feel lots of mixed emotions such as anxiousness, frustration and nervousness. Even though he found learning and studying challenging, he worked extremely hard to pursue his passion and become very famous in the field of acting.

"When you have to cope with a lot of problems, you're either going to sink or you're going to swim."

"My childhood was extremely lonely. I was dyslexic and lots of kids make fun of me. That experience made me tough inside, because you learn to quietly accept ridicule."

"I love what I do. I take great pride in what I do. And I can't do something halfway, three-quarters, nine-tenths. If I'm going to do something, I go all the way"

Daniel Radcliffe

English actor

Daniel Radcliffe started acting from the age of six, and by age 12 he became famous with the role of Harry Potter. He has publicly discussed that he suffers from mild dyspraxia. Radcliffe's main challenges with his dyspraxia were handwriting and tying his shoelaces up. Acting became his special talent, where he had no difficulty learning and remembering lines from scripts.

"It's mainly about working hard and proving to people you're serious about it and stretching yourself and learning."

"Working hard is important. But there is something that matters even more, believing in yourself."

"Go boldly and honestly through the world. Learn to love the fact that there is nobody else quite like you."

More Inspiring Quotes

Leonardo DiCaprio

American actor and film producer

Leonardo DiCaprio has disclosed his battles with OCD from when he was around 11-years-old. Some of his obsessive tendencies ranged from walking on the cracks of the footpath and knocking on the timber of a door-frame many times before entering a room. DiCaprio has found that positive self-talk is a strategy that works well for him.

"If you can do what you do best and be happy, you are further along in life than most people."

"I'm able to say at some point, okay, you're being ridiculous, stop stepping on every gum stain you see. You don't need to do that. You don't need to walk 20 feet back and put your foot on that thing. Nothing bad is going to happen."

"School, I never truly got the knack of. I could never focus on things I didn't want to learn. Math is just the worst. To this day, I can't concentrate on it. People always say, 'You should have tried harder.' But actually, I cheated a lot because I could not sit and do homework."

Sir Jackie Stewart

F1 racing driver

Jackie Stewart has a diagnosis of dyslexia and had a learning disability at school. He was labelled as being lazy, dumb and stupid, and was made fun of at school by his classmates. He was very good at using his hands and was a great mechanic – which he did before he went into F1 driving.

"The old Nürburgring had 187 corners per lap, and I can still give you every gear change, every braking distance on each of the 187 corners. But I can't say the alphabet."

"When faced with a challenge, embrace it as an opportunity for growth."

"Success is not measured by the trophies or accolades, but by the journey it takes to get there."

"Nobody's perfect, but all of us can be better than we are."

More Inspiring Quotes

Michael Phelps

Olympic swimmer

Olympic swimmer Michael Phelps was diagnosed with ADHD when he was about nine-years-old. Learning at school was a challenge, as he found it difficult to sit still in class and complete work within a specific time frame. The best form of therapy for him was swimming in a pool. This had a calming effect on him, which not only helped him to manage his ADHD, but also led to many successes at the Olympics.

"I had a teacher tell me that I would never amount to anything and I would never be successful."

"I saw kids who, we were all in the same class, and the teachers treated them differently than they would treat me."

"

The diagnosis made me want to prove everyone wrong. I knew that if I collaborated with Michael, he could achieve anything he set his mind too."
- Debbie Phelps, mom of Michael Phelps

Michael Jordan

NBA star

Michael Jordan was diagnosed with ADHD when he was a child. At school, this condition made it challenging for him to concentrate when learning. However, on the basketball court his hyperactivity not only gave him the ability to remain highly focussed, he was also able to display outstanding performances. Today, Jordan is highly regarded as one of the most well-known basketball players ever.

"Obstacles don't have to stop you. If you run into a wall, don't turn around and give up. Figure out how to climb it, go through it or work around it."

"Another day, another opportunity to prove everyone who doubt you wrong."

"I can accept failure, everyone fails at something. But I can't accept not trying."

More Inspiring Quotes

Tony Snell

NBA star veteran

Tony Snell was diagnosed with autism later in life, at age 31. His love for basketball not only kept him from potentially being involved in gangs, but his determination, focus and hard-working attitude gave him the opportunity to play for nine seasons in the NBA.

More about Tony's diagnosis can be watched on the following video: https://www.today.com/health/nba-star-tony-snell-speak-1st-time-autism-diagnosis-rcna89701

"I'm not a very emotional guy. I just move on to the next play. I've always been that way. I don't like showing much. I just try to do my job and get out. It's important to stay poised until that clock says zero."

"I was not surprised because I always felt different. I was just relieved, like this is why I am the way I am. It just made everything about my life make so much sense."

"Learning I have autism spectrum disorder (ASD) helped me understand my whole life" says Snell. *"This is why I am the way I am."*

Heath Shaw

AFL footballer

Shaw is one of the ambassadors for ADHD Australia, which is a wonderful opportunity to build awareness and share insights into what he has experienced.

Playing football and training sessions were the one place where he didn't notice his ADHD symptoms – it was an environment where he could flourish and reach his potential.

"I was average at school and diagnosed with ADHD in year eight. I find something I like I'll go a million miles an hour, if I don't like it then…"

More Inspiring Quotes

Katja Dedekind

World's fastest multi-class swimmer

Katja is a 'No Limits' Ambassador for the organisation FIGHT4BALANCE. In 2022 she became a world record holder in the women's 50-metre freestyle, S13 class. She was born in Durban, South Africa but grew up on the Gold Coast falling in love with Para-Olympic swimming where she trained alongside the Australian women's team.

"We all find something that makes us feel like everybody else"

"When I swim, I don't feel like I'm out of place, I feel like I actually fit in. I think without it I wouldn't have been able to grow into the person I am today."

Jamie Oliver

Celebrity chef and restauranteur

Jamie Oliver is a well-known British celebrity chef, who has been diagnosed with dyslexia. He has always found reading challenging, and it wasn't until at the age of 38 that he finished reading his first book. He has now gone on to have sold over 14.55 million of his own books!

"Being dyslexic is not an excuse for you not to prosper."

"School was a real struggle for me, people just thought I was thick. I really needed someone to help me understand my strengths."

"There are different types of intelligence and everyone has the ability to be brilliant."

Dylan Alcott

Australian Paralympian, guest speaker & media presenter

Dylan was born with his disability, and always had such a positive attitude which came from his positive experiences his family created for him. He loved being involved in sport, always trying his best to win. Through his involvement in sport Dylan's two passions became wheelchair basketball and tennis where he went on to win 15 grand slam singles events and 8 grand slam doubles titles. In the Paralympics he won 4 gold medals and 2 silver medals.

"People used to stare at me when I was growing up because I was in a wheelchair, and I hated it. Now they're staring at me because they know me. How amazing is that? It's 'Oh, that's Dylan!' Not, 'Oh, there's a guy in a wheelchair.'"

"Sport has really given me that platform and I love it, but now that I've got that I want to do it for everyone else with a disability."

Sarah Gordy

British actor

Sarah Gordy has Down syndrome, is an actor, dancer and is also a great supporter of Circus Starr. Her acting career has seen her in theatre productions, radio dramas, short films, television shows and commercials. Gordy is also the first woman with Down syndrome to be presented with an Order of the British Empire (MBE).

"Don't listen to doubts, don't listen to labels. Believe in yourself."

About the Author

More information about Jenny Cluning can be read in her other books, *Building Bright Futures* and *Educational Moves Reflex, Balance & Quick Reference Guide*.

As an author of two educational resource books, Jenny is a JIAS Provider, Early Movement Specialist, and trainer in professional development workshops.

Free information seminars

These are generally offered online approximately every six to eight weeks for interested parents / carers, educators, sports coaches and allied health professionals to gain a brief understanding of learning differences and options available for support. These seminars include:

- ◊ About Educational Moves
- ◊ What is Neurodevelopment delay?
- ◊ Understanding the importance of early movements
- ◊ Brief understanding of Primitive Reflexes and their effects if retained
- ◊ Brief understanding of Postural Reflexes and their effects if underdeveloped
- ◊ Ultimate Neurotherapies.

Professional development workshops

Workshop 1 - Fun exercises to support neurological development (no prerequisite to attend)

In this professional development learning workshop, you will learn fun exercises to support:

- ◊ Focus and concentration
- ◊ The sensory system
- ◊ Balance and motor coordination
- ◊ Social engagement.

Workshop 2 - Understanding Early Developmental and the Brain Movement Connections (no prerequisite to attend)

In this professional development workshop you will gain a deeper understanding of early development, motor development stages and how our brain is wired through movement.

Workshop 3 - Understanding Primitive and Postural Reflexes and the Sensory System (no pre requisite to attend)

In this workshop, you will gain a deeper understanding of the senses, along with primitive and postural reflexes.

Workshop 4 - Move to Learn Workshop (beneficial to have attended Workshops 2 and 3)

In this workshop, you will learn about:

- ◊ What is 'Move to Learn', and who founded the program
- ◊ Underlying causes of learning difficulties
- ◊ Developing a case history
- ◊ Learning and experiencing the movement from '10 Gems for the Brain'.

Workshop 5 - Introduction to Bilateral Integration (beneficial to have attended workshops 2, 3 & 4)

In this workshop, you will learn about:

- ◊ What is 'Bilateral Integration', and who founded the exercise program
- ◊ Bilateral Integration assessment testing
- ◊ Learning and experiencing the introductory exercises
- ◊ Combining 'Move to Learn' and 'Bilateral Integration' exercises.

To register your interest in attending a free information seminar, or one of the workshops, please contact Jenny via her email at educationalmoves@gmail.com, or through the website educationalmoves.com.au. The website has up to date information on all the professional development workshops regarding dates and costs.

Workshop testimonials

Mum of two boys, Registered teacher and Sound Therapy practitioner

I've just completed session one of Jenny's five-session online program. Today's session has made me feel a real sense of clarity and confidence that over the duration of the program, I will easily learn, integrate and embody new knowledge with practical skills. I'm grateful for the week in between so I can use the additional time to self-reflect and do further reading.

I'm so pleased I booked into learning online with you. The pace is perfect for me. Thanks again - today was wonderful!

Early childhood and early intervention co-ordinator

Jenny is an outstanding facilitator. Her training is so *real* and practical. It can be integrated into your and your child's everyday routines. The exercises I learnt are so much fun, and the video demonstrations are very clear. All I know about retained reflexes, how to integrate them and the effects they have on development I have learnt through Jenny.

I treasure the day I was introduced to her. She is so knowledgeable and approachable. I am so looking forward to learning more about neurodiversity through this book.

Senior osteopath & advanced paediatric osteopath – director of Growing Bones

Jenny's courses are really easy to understand and implement. She has a great ability to bring things back to basics – which removes barriers to putting it into practice.

I've already started using some of the things I've learnt on her last course, and the kids are very receptive and happy to do it! So different to other home exercises!

Newsletters & free neurodevelopmental exercises

To subscribe to Educational Moves monthly newsletters and access to six fun bean bag / ball exercises, please visit our website for more details through the QR code below.

Acknowledgments

Firstly, special thanks must go to Abby Harvey for her editing expertise, and to everyone at Busybird Publishing for their management, cover design, expert advice, guidance and support in publishing my third book.

Utmost gratitude to my dear friend and colleague Glynis Brummer, Dip.Teaching, B.Ed, M.Ed (Special Ed) from Smart Learning Solutions in New Zealand for taking the time to write the foreword for this book.

Very special thank you to my friend and colleague Aphrodite Zoitas, Psychologist, B.App.Sc.(Psych) (Hons), M.Psych., Grad.Dip. Disability Studies, MAPS for previewing this book and offering her advice on neurodiverse conditions.

I want to express my gratitude to Julie Fisher, mother, author, keynote speaker and disability advocate, for contributing her special story at the beginning of this book on herself and son Darcy. Special thanks to Stephanie Rodden Photography for the photo of Julie and Darcy on page iv.

So grateful for the useful feedback from Karen Dymke, Education Consultant, Facilitator, Coach, Masters Ed. BEd, Dip T, Cert 1V TAE. Your knowledge and experience in the area of learning styles has been invaluable.

Special thank you to Sue Dymond from SD Connect for taking the time to put together her delightful story titled *My Balloon Girl*.

Sincere appreciation to Vanessa Nicoletti for her hand drawn image on page 49. Vanessa originally drew this picture for my first book, *Building Bright Futures*.

My heartfelt thanks to those who took the time to write about their positive experience from attending one of my professional development workshops.

Utmost thanks to Sandra Garvey for her creative artwork of the brain pictured in Sections 1 and 5.

References

Section 1 - Understanding Neurodiversity

» **NHS Cambridge University Hospitals, What is Neurodiversity,** https://www.cuh.nhs.uk/our-people/neurodiversity-at-cuh/what-is-neurodiversity/

» **Cleveland Clinic, Executive Dysfunction,** https://my.clevelandclinic.org/health/symptoms/23224-executive-dysfunction

» **Wikipedia The Free Encyclopedia, Cognitive disorder,** https://en.wikipedia.org/wiki/Cognitive_disorder

» **NIH, National Library of Medicine, Dysgraphia,** https://www.ncbi.nlm.nih.gov/books/NBK559301/

» **Merriam Webster Dictionary, neurodiverse,** https://www.merriam-webster.com/dictionary/neurodiverse

» **Understood, What is Slow Processing Speed?,** https://www.understood.org/en/articles/processing-speed-what-you-need-to-know

» **Mayo Clinic, Stuttering,** https://www.mayoclinic.org/diseases-conditions/stuttering/symptoms-causes/syc-20353572#:~:text=Stuttering%20%E2%80%94%20also%20called%20stammering%20or,but%20have%20difficulty%20saying%20it.

» **CDC, Tourette Syndrome,** https://www.cdc.gov/tourette-syndrome/about/index.html

- » **Lincoln Land Community College, Characteristics of Learn-ing Styles,** https://www.llcc.edu/center-academic-success/helpful-resources/characteristics-learning-styles

- » Video Link: https://www.brainfacts.org/core-concepts/how-your-brain-processes-information

- » **Science Direct, Multimedia Learning,** https://www.sciencedirect.com/topics/economics-econometrics-and-finance/multimedia-learning#:~:text=Richard%20Mayer's%20research%20in%20multimedia,that%20each%20reinforces%20the%20other

Learning Styles

- » **Education Next, The Stubborn Myth of "Learning Styles",** The Stubborn Myth of "Learning Styles" - Education Next, https://www.educationnext.org/wp-content/uploads/2022/01/ednext_XX_3_furey.pdf

- » **Go1, Learning And Development, Are learning styles a myth or valid?,** https://www.go1.com/blog/myth-learning-styles

- » **FEE, Foundation for Economic Education, Learning Styles Don't Actually Exist, Studies Show,** https://fee.org/articles/learning-styles-don-t-actually-exist-studies-show/#:~:text=%E2%80%9CThere%20is%20no%20credible%20evidence,will%20lead%20to%20better%20learning.%E2%80%9D

- » **Don't Believe Everything You Think, Learning Styles and the Importance of Critical Self-Regulation, Tesha Marshik,** https://www.youtube.com/watch?v=855Now8h5Rs

- » **(TEDx Talk video,** *Learning Styles & the importance of critical self-reflection / Tesia Marshik / TEDxuWLaCrosse)*

- » **Andy Matuschak, Andy's working notes, Chase and Simon – Perception in chess,** https://notes.andymatuschak.org/Chase_and_Simon_-_Perception_in_chess?ref=josephnoelwalker.com

- » **Recall memory for visually presented chess positions PETER W. FREY and PETER ADESMAN Northwestern**

References

University, Evanston, Illi7W'is 60201, https://link.springer.com/content/pdf/10.3758/bf03213216.pdf

» **DevEd by Kamran Yyub, Learning styles are a myth, part 3,** https://kamranayub.com/learning-styles-3/

Section 2 – 7 Common Conditions

Autism Spectrum Disorder (ASD)

» **National Institute of Mental Health, Autism Spectrum Disorder,** https://www.nimh.nih.gov/health/topics/autism-spectrum-disorders-asd

» **National institute on Deafness and other Communication Disorders, Autism SpectrumDisorder: Communication Problems in Children,** https://www.nidcd.nih.gov/health/autism-spectrum-disorder-communication-problems-children

» **raising children.net.au the australian parenting website, Autism: What is it?,** https://raisingchildren.net.au/autism/learning-about-autism/about-autism/asd-overview

» **Better Health Channel, Autism and Adults,** https://www.betterhealth.vic.gov.au/health/conditionsandtreatments/autism-spectrum-disorder-and-adults

» **Kerry Magro, 12 Dr Seuss Quotes That Inspire Me as an Autism Advocate,** https://kerrymagro.com/12-dr-seuss-quotes-that-inspire-our-disability-community/

» **Communication Hub – connect . learn . access, strategies to help communication,** https://www.speechpathologyaustralia.org.au/Communication_Hub/Resources/Fact_Sheets/Intellectual_disability.aspx

» **Nurse Next Door, home car3 services**, https://www.nursenextdoor.com.au/blog/how-to-communicatewith-

» people-with-intellectual-disabilities/#effectively-communicate

- » **autism speaks, Medical Conditions Associated with ASD,** https://www.autismspeaks.org/medical-conditions-associated-autism#:~:text=Attention%2Ddeficit%2Fhyperactivity%20disorder%20(,Obsessive%20compulsive%20disorder%20(OCD)

- » **Ernie Els, Els for Autism, 30 quotes from 30 people with Autism,** https://www.elsforautism.org/30-quotes-from-30-people-with-autism/

- » **FIT, the quint world, Dan Aykrod,** https://www.thequint.com/fit/celebrities-autism-aspergers-syndrome-world-autism-awareness-day-courtney-love-einstein-susan-boyle-2

- » **MentalHelp.net, Special Autistic Abilities (Savant Behaviour),** https://www.mentalhelp.net/autism/special-abilities-savant-behavior/#:~:text=Mathematical%2C%20artistic%2C%20musical%2C%20spatial,usually%20involves%20a%20remarkable%20memory.

- » **Autism Speaks, 10 inspiring quotes from people with Autism,** https://www.autismspeaks.org/life-spectrum/10-inspiring-quotes-people-autism

Attention Deficit Hyperactive Disorder (ADHD)

- » **Lifestyle, 7 most common neurodivergent conditions,** https://longevity.technology/lifestyle/7-most-common-neurodivergent-conditions/

- » **Centers for Disease Control and Prevention, What is ADHD?,** https://www.cdc.gov/adhd/index.html

- » **Healthline, Common Signs of Attention Deficit Hyperactive Disorder (ADHD),** https://www.healthline.com/health/adhd/signs

- » **Psych Central, Do I Have ADHD? 8 Subtle Signs in Adults,** https://psychcentral.com/adhd/subtle-signs-you-may-have-adult-adhd

- » **National Library of Medicine, Mapping phenotypic and aetiological associations between ADHD and physical conditions in adulthood in Sweden: a genetically informed register study,** https://pubmed.ncbi.nlm.nih.gov/34242595/

- » **Centers for Disease Control and Prevention, Other Concerns and Conditions with ADHD,** https://www.cdc.gov/adhd/articles/helping-children-with-multiple-concerns.html

- » **Verywellmind, Improving Communication with your child with ADHD,** https://www.verywellmind.com/parenting-adhd-children-parenting-strategies-20543

- » **WedMED, Communication Hacks for ADHD,** https://www.webmd.com/add-adhd/adhd-communication-hacks

- » **Healthline, 9 Celebrities with ADHD,** https://www.healthline.com/health/adhd/celebrities

Intellectual Disability

- » **Centers for Disease Control and Prevention, Facts about Intellectual Disability,** https://www.cdc.gov/ncbddd/developmentaldisabilities/facts-about-intellectual-disability.html#:~:text=Intellectual%20disability%20is%20a%20term,disability%20vary%20greatly%20in%20children.

- » **Inclusion Australia, What is Intellectual Disability,** https://www.inclusionaustralia.org.au/intellectual-disability/what-is-intellectual-disability/#:~:text=Intellectual%20disability%20is%20a%20lifelong,emotional%20skills%20and%20physical%20skills.

- » **MILLCREEK, Signs & Symptoms of Intellectual Disabilities,** https://www.millcreekofmagee.com/disorders/intellectual-disability/signs-causes-symptoms/

- » **ECCM, Signs of Intellectual Disability in Adults,** https://www.eccm.org/blog/signs-of-intellectual-disabilities-in-adults

- » **Voice Your Stories, Inspiring Quotes For Disability,** https://www.voiceyourstories.com/inspiring-quotes-for-disability/

Dyslexia

» **Better Health Channel, Dyslexia,** https://www.betterhealth.vic.gov.au/health/conditionsandtreatments/dyslexia

» **Cleveland Clinic, Dyslexia,** https://my.clevelandclinic.org/health/diseases/6005-dyslexia

» **British Dyslexia Association, Am I dyslexic?,** https://www.bdadyslexia.org.uk/advice/adults/am-i-dyslexic

» **Dyslexic Support South, Strengths of Dyslexia,** https://www.dyslexiasupportsouth.org.nz/parent-toolkit/emotional-impact/strengths-of-dyslexia/#:~:text=Dyslexic%20strengths%20include%3A&text=%EF%82%B7%20High%20levels%20of%20empathy,%EF%82%B7%20Strong%20narrative%20reasoning

» **Number Dyslexia,** 6 Ways To Effectively Communicate With A Person With Dyslexia - Number Dyslexia

» **Fairfax County Public Schools, Common Co-Existing Conditions with Dyslexia,** https://www.fcps.edu/academics/academic-overview/special-education-instruction/high-incidence-disabilities-team-k-12-16#:~:text=Some%20students%20with%20dyslexia%20also,disorder%2C%20and%2For%20anxiety

Quotes:

» https://wecapable.com/disability-quotes-inspiring-words/

» https://www.bookbotkids.com/blog/dyslexia-quotes

» https://quotefancy.com/daniel-radcliffe-quotes

» https://www.brainyquote.com/authors/chris-burke-quotes

Dyspraxia

» **Healthdirect, Dyspraxia,** https://www.healthdirect.gov.au/dyspraxia

» **High Speed Training, How Does Dyspraxia Affect Adults?,** https://www.highspeedtraining.co.uk/hub/how-does-dyspraxia-affect-adults/

References

- **Exceptional Individuals, Common Dyspraxia Traits,** https://exceptionalindividuals.com/neurodiversity/what-is-dyspraxia/#:~:text=Common%20Dyspraxia%20strengths&text=Dyspraxics%20often%20learn%20to%20develop,in%20dyspraxics%20making%20good%20leaders.

- **Scottish Acquired Brain Injury Network, ABI eLearning Resource, How to Help the Person with Communication Impairments Arising from Dyspraxia,** https://www.acquiredbraininjury-education.scot.nhs.uk/impact-of-abi/communication-problems/communication-and-dyspraxia/how-to-help-the-person-with-dyspraxia/

- **NHS, Dyspraxia (developmental coordination disorder) in adults,** https://www.nhs.uk/conditions/developmental-coordination-disorder-dyspraxia-in-adults/#:~:text=If%20you%20have%20dyspraxia%2C%20you,autism%20spectrum%20disorder

- https://www.health.qld.gov.au/__data/assets/pdf_file/0032/674177/dyspraxia_strategies_pro.pdf

Dyscalculia

- **IDL, Superpowers of Dyscalculia, 6 Superpowers of Dyscalculia,** https://idlsgroup.com/news/superpowers-of-dyscalculia/#:~:text=Problem%20Solving%20%E2%80%93%20people%20with%20dyscalculia,at%20reading%20writing%20and%20spelling.

- **Brain Balance, 5 strategies for managing Dyscalculia,** https://www.brainbalancecenters.com/blog/strategies-for-managing-dyscalculia

- **ADDITUDE Celebrating 25 Years, Famous People with Dyslexia, Dyscalculia & other Learning Differences,** https://www.additudemag.com/slideshows/famous-people-with-dyslexia-learning-differences/#:~:text=Singer%2C%20Actor%20with%20Dyscalculia&text=%E2%80%9CI%20couldn't%20read%20quickly,had%20to%20learn%20by%20listening.

- **Cleveland Clinic, Dyscalculia,** https://my.clevelandclinic.org/health/diseases/23949-dyscalculia

Dysgraphia

- **Exceptional Individuals, Dysgraphia,** https://exceptionalindividuals.com/neurodiversity/what-is-dysgraphia/#strengths

- **SPELD NSW,** *Supporting children and adults with specific learning difficulties,* https://www.speldnsw.org.au/information/dysgraphia/#:~:text=Dysgraphia%20is%20a%20difficulty%20with,learning%20disorder%20in%20written%20expression.

- **Touch-Type Read & Spell, 9 strategies for dysgraphia,** https://www.readandspell.com/strategies-for-dysgraphia

- **North Shore Paediatric Therapy, Developmental Milestones for Pre-Writing and Writing Skills,** https://www.nspt4kids.com/parenting/developmental-milestones-pre-writing-writing-skills#:~:text=6%20years%3A%20Typically%2C%20children%20should,letters%20without%20switching%20forms%20throughout.

Section 3 – Communication Strategies

- **Medium, Why Do Neurodivergent People Have Quirky Special Interests?,** https://medium.com/illumination/why-do-neurodivergent-people-have-quirky-special-interests-fde0f6365822

- **Prospect, I manage someone who is neurodivergent—what can I do to support them?,** https://prospect.org.uk/article/i-manage-someone-who-is-neurodiverse-what-can-i-do-to-support-them/

- **Learning Tools, Coaching Dyslexics, Getting Through to Your Dyslexic Athletes,** https://learningtoolsforlife.com/coaching-dyslexics/

- **LinkedIn, Dyslexic Thinking in Action, 5 reasons Dyslexic thinking makes unstoppable sports champions,** https://www.linkedin.com/pulse/5-reasons-dyslexic-thinking-makes-unstoppable-sports-champions-kate

Section 4 – Supporting Neurodiversity (Auditory Stimulation)

- **Linkedin, Tomatis New Zealand's Post,** https://www.linkedin.com/posts/tomatisnz_tomatis-tomatismethod-apd-activity-7228841517577031681-esXA/

- **Mighty Minds and Muscles, Tomatis – A Listening Program,** https://www.mightymindsandmuscles.com/tomatis---a-listening-program

- **Smart Learning Solutions, The JIAS (Sound Therapy) Programme, Johasnen Individualised Auditory Stimulation,** https://www.smartlearning.co.nz/jias-sound-therapy

- **Johansen IAS, The Johansen Story,** https://johansenias.com/about-us/johansen-story/

- **Johansen IAS, Research,** https://johansenias.com/about-jias/research/

- **MPC High Tech Centre, Tomatis,** http://www.htcmpc.org/tomatis.html

Section 5 – Stories and Inspiring Quotes

Albert Einstein

- **BrainyQuote, Albert Einstein Quotes,** https://www.brainyquote.com/authors/albert-einstein-quotes

- **Washington Parent, 21 People who succeeded despite a learning disability, Albert Einstein,** https://washingtonparent.com/21-people-who-succeeded-despite-a-learning-disability/#:~:text=Albert%20Einstein&text=He%20didn't%20learn%20to,for%20his%20theory%20of%20relativity.

- » **"Exceptional Individuals, Was Albert Einstein Autistic, Dyslexic, Dyspraxic or have ADHD?,** https://exceptionalindividuals.com/about-us/blog/did-einstein-have-dyslexia-dyspraxia-autism-and-adhd/

Dan Aykroyd

- » **Ernie Els, Elms for Autism, 30 Quotes from 30 People with Autism,** https://www.elsforautism.org/30-quotes-from-30-people-with-autism/

- » **24 Quirky Dan Aykroyd Quotes, by Autism Inked, Sept 14, 2023, Autism & Aspergers Quotes,** https://autisminked.com/24-quirky-dan-aykroyd-quotes/

- » **ADDITUDE Celebrating 25 Years, 10 ADHD Quotes to Save for a Bad Day,** https://www.additudemag.com/slideshows/adhd-quotes-for-a-bad-day/

Michael Phelps

- » **People, Michael Phelps Opens Up About ADHD Struggles: A Teacher Told Me 'I'd Never Amount to Anything',** https://people.com/sports/michael-phelps-opens-up-about-adhd-struggles-in-new-video-a-teacher-told-me-id-never-amount-to-anything/

Michael Jordan

- » **Coordikids, Michael Jordan,** https://www.coordikids.com/famous-people-with-adhd/

- » **Brainy Quote, Michael Jordan Quotes,** https://www.brainyquote.com/quotes/michael_jordan_385092

Tom Cruise

- » **the Reading Well, A Virtual Well of Dyslexic Resources, Successful People with Dyslexia: Tom Cruise,** https://www.dyslexia-reading-well.com/tom-cruise.html#:~:text=%E2%80%9CWhen%20I%20was%20about%207,I%20would%20get%20angry.

References

- the Reading Well, A virtual well of dyslexia resources, Successful People with Dyslexia: Tom Cruise, https://www.dyslexia-reading-well.com/tom-cruise.html#:~:text=Quotes,learn%20to%20quietly%20accept%20ridicule.%E2%80%9D

Daniel Radcliffe

- Understood, "Harry Potter" Star Gives Dyspraxia Advice, https://www.understood.org/en/articles/harry-potter-star-gives-dyspraxia-advice

- abc News, Dyspraxia Explains Harry Potter's Klutziness, https://abcnews.go.com/Health/story?id=5605093&page=1#:~:text=But%2C%20asking%20him%20to%20tie,disorder%20commonly%20associated%20with%20klutziness.

- AZ Quotes, Daniel Radcliffe Quotes, https://www.azquotes.com/author/12009-Daniel_Radcliffe

- Wikipedia The Free Encyclopedia, Daniel Radcliffe, https://en.wikipedia.org/wiki/Daniel_Radcliffe

Leonardo DiCaprio

- Choosing Therapy, 3. Leonardo DiCaprio, https://www.choosingtherapy.com/famous-people-with-ocd/

- GoalCast, Top 12 Most Inspiring Leonardo DiCaprio Quotes, https://www.goalcast.com/top-12-inspiring-leonardo-dicaprio-quotes/

- Serenity Mental Health Centers, Celebrities with Mental Illnesses Speak Out to End Stigma, https://serenitymentalhealthcenters.com/articles/celebrities-with-mental-illness-speak-out-to-end-stigma/

Katja Dedekind

- Paralympics Australia, Katja Dedkind, https://www.paralympic.org.au/imagine/katja-dedekind/

- » **F4B, OUR AMBASSADORS, Katja Dedekind: 'Fastest World Multiclass Swimmer in history'**, https://www.fight4balance.org.au/ambassadors

Heath Shaw

- » **Matific, ADHD in our Classrooms, Heath Shaw's ADHD Experience,** https://www.matific.com/au/en-au/home/blog/2022/03/07/conversation-heath-shaw-afl-star-adhd-story/

- » https://www.dailymail.co.uk/tvshowbiz/article-10016229/SAS-Australia-Heath-Shaw-breaks-discusses-diagnosis.html

Justin Timberlake

- » **Choosing Therapy, 6. Justin Timberlake,** https://www.choosingtherapy.com/famous-people-with-ocd/

Sir Jackie Stewart

- » **The Yale Centre for Dyslexia & Creativity, Sir Jackie Stewart, World Champion Race Car Driver,** https://dyslexia.yale.edu/story/sir-jackie-stewart/#:~:text=Jackie%20Stewart%20would%20finally%20receive,arm%20to%20a%20drowning%20man.

- » **Independent, Jackie Stewart on a life with dyslexia and his unrelenting push for safety in Formula 1,** https://www.independent.co.uk/f1/jackie-stewart-dyslexia-jochen-rindt-francois-cevert-b2252462.html

- » **BooKey, 30 Best Jackie Stewart Quotes With Image,** https://www.bookey.app/quote-author/jackie-stewart

Tony Snell

- » **BrainyQuote,** https://www.brainyquote.com/quotes/tony_snell_832130

- » **Today, NBA star Tony Snell speaks out for 1st time on autism diagnosis: "I am the way I am",** https://www.today.com/health/nba-star-tony-snell-speak-1st-time-autism-diagnosis-rcna89701

References

» **Special Olympics, In the News, Tim Shriver and Tony Snell Speak Up for Parents of Children with Intellectual Disabilities,** https://www.specialolympics.org/stories/news/tim-shriver-and-tony-snell-speak-up-for-parents-of-children-with-intellectual-disabilities

Sarah Gordy

» **IMDb, Sarah Gordy Biography,** https://www.imdb.com/name/nm1527688/bio/

» **The Indian Express, Journalism of Courage, "Don't listen to doubts, don't listen to labels. Believe in Yourself",** https://indianexpress.com/article/lifestyle/life-positive/dont-listen-to-doubt-dont-listen-to-labels-believe-in-yourself-sarah-gordy-5764004/

» **Circus Starr, the circus with a purpose, Our Patron, Sarah Gordy MBE, Stage and Screen Actress,** https://www.circus-starr.org.uk/our-patron/

Dylan Alcott

» **Britannica, Dylan Alcott, Australian basketball and tennis player, Switch to tennis,** https://www.britannica.com/sports/Australian-rules-football/Rise-of-the-Victorian-Football-League

» **BrainyQuote,** https://www.brainyquote.com/authors/dylan-alcott-quotes

Jamie Oliver

» **Facebook,** https://www.facebook.com/bbcbreakfast/videos/jamie-oliver-talks-about-living-with-dyslexia/990733488582846/

http://www.educationalmoves.com.au/

www.ingramcontent.com/pod-product-compliance
Lightning Source LLC
Chambersburg PA
CBHW062039290426
44109CB00026B/2678